William B. Bradbury

Marching Along

The popular Army song and chorus

William B. Bradbury

Marching Along
The popular Army song and chorus

ISBN/EAN: 9783337350734

Printed in Europe, USA, Canada, Australia, Japan

Cover: Foto ©Thomas Meinert / pixelio.de

More available books at **www.hansebooks.com**

MARCHING ALONG

THE POPULAR

Army Song and Chorus

BY

WM. B. BRADBURY.

2½

NEW YORK
Published by FIRTH. POND &CO. 547 Broadway

Boston
O.DITSON &CO.

Cincinnati.
C.Y.FONDA.

Pittsburgh
H.KLEBER & BRO.

"MARCHING ALONG."

(ARMY SONG.)

Words adapted by Mrs M. A. KIDDER.　　　　Music composed by W. B. BRADBURY.

The Ar - my is gath'ring from near and from far, The trum - pet is sound-ing the

call for the war; M'Clel - lan's our lead - er, he's gal - lant and strong, We'll

8213

girl on our armor, and be march-ing a-long! March-ing a-long, we are march-ing a-long, Gird on the ar-mor and be march-ing a-long: M'c Clel-lan's our lead-er, he's gal-lant and strong, For God and our country we are march-ing along.

2

The foe is before us in battle array
But let us not waver, or turn from the way;
The Lord is our strength, and the Union's our song,
With courage and faith, we are marching along.
　　　　　Marching along (&c.)

3

Our wives and our children we leave in your care,
We feel you will help them their sorrows to bear;
'Tis hard has to part, but we hope 'twont be long.
We'll keep up our hearts as we're marching along.
　　　　　Marching along (&c.)

4

We sigh for our country, we mourn for our dead,
For them now our last drop of blood we will shed:
Our cause is the right one— our foe's in the wrong,
Then gladly we'll sing as we're marching along.
　　　　　Marching along (&c.)

5

The Flag of our country is floating on high,
We'l stand by that Flag till we conquer or die;
M'cClellan's our leader, he's gallant and strong,
Will gird on our armor, and be marching along.
　　　　　Marching along (&c.)

CHORUS.

Sopr'o. Match-ing a-long, we are marching a-long, Gird on the armor and be march ing a-long; Me

Alto.

Tenor. March-ing a-long, we are marching a-long, Gird on the armor and be march ing a-long; Me

Bass.

Piano.

Clel - lan's our lead - er, he's gal - lant and strong, For God and our country we are march - ing a - long!

Clel - lan's our lead - er, he's gal - lant and strong, For God and our country we are march - ing a - long!

Clayton.

The Battle-Cry of Freedom.

SONG and CHORUS by Geo. F. Root.

CHICAGO:

PUBLISHED BY ROOT & CADY.

95 CLARK STREET.

THE BATTLE-CRY OF FREEDOM.

(BATTLE SONG.)

I.

We are marching to the field, boys, we're going to the fight,
  Shouting the battle-cry of freedom,
And we bear the glorious stars for the Union and the right,
  Shouting the battle-cry of freedom.

> CHORUS.—The Union forever, Hurrah! boys, Hurrah!
>   Down with the traitor, up with the star,
> For we're marching to the field boys, going to the fight,
>   Shouting the battle-cry of freedom!

II.

We will meet the rebel host, boys, with fearless heart and true,
  Shouting the battle-cry of freedom,
And we'll show what Uncle Sam has for loyal men to do,
  Shouting the battle-cry of freedom.

> CHORUS.—The Union forever, etc.

III.

If we fall amid the fray, boys, we'll face them to the last,
  Shouting the battle-cry of freedom,
And our comrades brave shall hear us, as they go rushing past,
  Shouting the battle-cry of freedom.

> CHORUS.—The Union forever. etc.

IV.

Yes, for Liberty and Union we're springing to the fight,
  Shouting the battle-cry of freedom,
And the vict'ry shall be ours, for we're rising in our might,
  Shouting the battle-cry of freedom.

> CHORUS.—The Union forever, etc.

THE BATTLE CRY OF FREEDOM.

RALLYING SONG.

GEO. F. ROOT.

INTRODUCTION.

1. Yes we'll ral - ly round the flag, boys, we'll
2. We are spring - ing to the call of our
3. We will wel - come to our num - bers the
4. So we're spring - ing to the call from the

ral - ly once a - gain, Shouting the bat - tle - cry of Free - dom, We will
Broth - ers gone be - fore, Shouting the bat - tle - cry of Free - dom, And we'll
loy - al true and brave, Shouting the bat - tle - cry of Free - dom, And al -
East and from the West, Shouting the bat - tle - cry of Free - dom, And we'll

ral - ly from the hill - side, we'll gath-er from the plain, Shout - ing the bat - tle - cry of

fill the va - cant ranks with a million free - men more, Shout - ing the bat - tle - cry of

tho' they may be poor not a man shall be a slave, Shout - ing the bat - tle - cry of

hurl the reb - el crew from the land we love the best, Shout - ing the bat - tle - cry of

CHORUS.

Fortissimo.

Air.

Free - dom. The Un - ion for - ev - er, Hur - rah boys, Hur-rah!

Alto.

The Un - ion for - ev - er, Hur - rah boys, Hur-rah!

Tenor.

The Un - ion for - ev - er, Hur - rah boys, Hur-rah!

Base.

The Un - ion for - ev - er, Hur - rah boys, Hur-rah!

335-4

Down with the trai - tor, Up with the star; While we ral - ly round the flag, boys,

Down with the trai - tor, Up with the star; While we ral - ly round the flag, boys,

Down with the trai - tor, Up with the star; While we ral - ly round the flag, boys,

Ral - ly once a - gain, Shout - ing the bat - tle - cry of Free - dom.

Ral - ly once a - gain, Shout - ing the bat - tle - cry of Free - dom.

Ral - ly once a - gain, Shout - ing the bat - tle - cry of Free - dom.

CIRCULAR LIST OF CIRCULATING PUBLICATIONS.

ROOT & CADY,
CHICAGO, Clark Street.
95
PUBLISHERS.

HOW TO GET OUR PUBLICATIONS.— If not found at the nearest Music Store, write directly to us.

O wrap the Flag around me. Taylor....25cts.
Vacant Chair. Root....25cts.
The Old House far away. Merrill....25cts.
Vesper Song for our Volunteers Singers. 25cts.
Who'll save the Left? Root....50cts.
Little Major, the Drummer Boy. Work..25cts.
Song of a Thousand Years. Work....25cts.
Polka Gracieuse. Wm. Mason....60cts.
The Days when We were Young. Work. 25cts.
Sixty-Three is the Jubilee. French...25cts.
Stand Up for Uncle Sam. Root....25cts.
Singular Dreams—comic. Dodge.....25cts.
Take your Gun and Go, John. Merrill. 25cts.
Tread Lightly ye Comrades. Crane...25cts.
Oh, Haste to Sleep, Mother. Root....25cts.
Rock me to Sleep on the Battle. Root...50cts.
Marie Polka Mazurka. Wollenhaupt. 50cts.
The Dear Ones all at Home. Bradbury. 25cts.
First Love Dream. Work....25cts.
Day of Liberty's Coming. Work....25cts.
Kingdom Coming. Work....35cts.
Battle-Cry of Freedom. Root....35cts.
Rock Me to Sleep Transcription. Stead. 75cts.
President's Emancipation March....30cts.
Gen. McClernand's Grand March....35cts.
Battle-Cry of Freedom War. Rein....60cts.
Kingdom Coming Variations. Grobe. 60cts.
Mine is the Mourning Heart. Foster. 25cts.
Grafted into the Army. Work....35cts.
He's Coming Again. Arr. by Root....35cts.
Jenny's Coming Home. Arr. by Root. 35cts.
I am dying. I pray. 35cts.
O wrap the Flag around me. Taylor....25cts.

TRAMP! TRAMP! TRAMP! or the— PRISONER'S HOPE.

AS SUNG BY EDWIN KELLEY,
OF ARLINGTON KELLEY & LEON'S MINSTRELS.

Song & Chorus.

BY GEO. F. ROOT.

Published by Root & Cady.
67 Washington St.
CHICAGO.

TRAMP! TRAMP! TRAMP!

(THE PRISONER'S HOPE.)

Tempo di Marcia. Words and Music By GEO. F. ROOT.

PIANO.

1. In the pris-on cell I sit, Think-ing Moth-er dear, of you, And our
2. In the bat-tle front we stood When their fierc-est charge they made, And they
3. So with-in the pris-on cell, We are wait-ing for the day That shall

bright and hap-py home so far a-way, And the tears they fill my eyes Spite of
swept us off a hun-dred men or more, But be-fore we reach'd their lines They were
come to o-pen wide the i-ron door, And the hol-low eye grows bright, And the

NEW METHOD FOR THE PIANO-FORTE

240 pp. Royal Quarto.

THE MUSICAL

CURRICULUM

BY GEO. F. ROOT.

THIS is emphatically a new book in a new field. It provides instruction and music, not only for the PIANO-FORTE, but also for the things that should be studied with it, viz; the VOICE and HARMONY—not harmony through the eye, but harmony through the ear ; not dry calculations, but living and beautiful forms. It goes on the plan that the pupil should know as well the chords and harmonies he is in while playing and singing, as he does the key or kind of time ; and moreover it proves that these things can be done by preparing well for each subject, and then by adapting the instruction, and the music to the state of the pupil, and making the steps succeed each other in true progressive order.

The whole book may be divided into two kinds of lessons—the one for *musical* culture and the other for *muscular* culture. Not that there is no practice for the muscles in the former, nor exercise for the musical taste in the latter, but each is devoted mainly to its own object. Those lessons which are designed to awaken, develop, and strengthen a love for music, and with which are imparted a knowledge of time, tune, and expression, (Rhythmics, Melodies, and Dynamics,) are written in many pleasant and tuneful forms, and are called *exercises, pieces, songs, études, solfeggios,* etc.,

while those which are simply for the development and strengthening of the muscles of the fingers, hands, and vocal organs, do not pretend to be pleasant or tuneful, but depend upon the benefits they confer in the way of flexibility and execution, for their popularity. These lessons are called TECHNICS, and embrace *five finger exercises, scales, arpeggios, and miscellaneous exercises* of many kinds and forms.

The contents of the book may be summed up as follows :

Price $4.50.

Sent, postpaid, on receipt of the marked price.

To those who would like to have an opportunity of examining this book before purchasing, we will send, postpaid, on receipt of ten cents, an elegant royal quarto pamphlet, containing fourteen specimen pages of the same, selected so as to give an idea of its general appearance, as well as some description of its plan and contents.

ROOT & CADY,   CHICAGO.

BEN BOLT.

OH! DON'T YOU REMEMBER.

Sung by
MISS CLARA BRUCE.

Composed by
NELSON KNEASS.

1138 *Piano* 3c *cts. net.*   1371 *Guitar* 25 *cts. net.*

Published by W. C. PETERS & SONS, Cincinnati.
Baltimore, W. C. PETERS,—PETERS, WEBB & CO., Louisville.
BALMER & WEBER, St. Louis.
WM. T. MAYO, New Orleans.

BEN BOLT,

or

OH! DON'T YOU REMEMBER.

As Sung by J.H. M⁰CANN.   The Music by N. KNEASS.

Oh! don't you remember sweet Alice, Ben Bolt – Sweet Alice with hair so brown, She

wept with delight when you gave her a smile, And trembled with fear at your frown. In the

1132

4

old church yard, in the valley, Ben Bolt, In a corner obscure and a - lone, They have

fitted a slab of granite so gray, And sweet Alice lies un - der the stone. They have

Ad libitum.

fitted a slab of granite so gray, And sweet Alice lies un - der the stone.

Ad libitum.

Ben Bolt. 1138 - 5.

3d ver: Oh! don't you remember the school, Ben Bolt, And the Mas - ter so kind and so
2d ver: Oh! don't you remember the wood, Ben Bolt, Near the green sunny slope of the
true, And the lit - tle nook by the clear running brook, Where we
hill, Where oft we have sung 'neath its wide spreading shade, And kept
gath - er'd the flow'rs as they grew. On the Mas - - - ter's grave grows the
time to the click of the mill: The mill has gone to de -
grass, Ben Bolt, And the running lit-tle brook is now dry; And of
- cay, Ben Bolt, And a qui - - et now reigns all a - round, See the

all the friends who were school mates then, There re — mains Ben, but you and

old rus-tic porch with its roses so sweet, Lies scatter'd and fallen to the

I. And of all the friends who were school mates then, There re -

ground, See the old rustic porch, with its roses so sweet, Lies

mains Ben, but you and I.

Ad libitum.

scatter'd and fallen to the ground.

Ad libitum.

E.H. Andrews Printer.

FADING STILL FADING.

AN

EVENING HYMN

Arranged for the

Piano Forte

Adapted to a Celebrated

PORTUGUESE MELODY.

Philadelphia, J. C. SMITH, 245 Chesnut St.

Andante.

Fa _ ding, still fa _ ding, the last beam is shi _ ning,

Fa _ ther, in hea _ ven the day is de _ cli _ ning; Safe _ ty and

in _ nocence fly with the light, Temp _ ta _ tion and dan _ ger walk forth with the night, From the fall of the shade till the morn _ ing bells

chime, Shield me from dan _ ger and save me from crime.

CHORUS.

Father have mercy, Father have mercy, Father have mercy thro' Jesus christ our Lord.

Father have mercy, Father have mercy, Father have mercy thro' Jesus christ our Lord.

2nd. VERSE.

Father in heaven, Oh! hear when we call.
Hear for Christ's sake who is Saviour of all,
Feeble and fainting we trust in thy might,
In doubting and darkness thy love be our light;
Let us sleep on thy breast while the nigt taper burns,
And wake in thy arms when the morning returns.

Father have mercy &c.

The last beam is shining. 9.

The last beam is shining

AN
EVENING HYMN

Arranged for the Piano Forte.

FROM A CELEBRATED
Portuguese Melody.

Philad.ª Published by G.E.Blake,13 south Fifth street.

Fa _ ding still fa _ ding the last beam is shi _ ning,

Fa _ ther in hea _ ven the day is de _ cli _ ning, Safe _ ty and

in _ no _ cence fly with the light, Temp _ ta _ tion and dan _ ger walk forth with the night, From the fall of the shade till the morn ing bells

chime, Shield me from danger and save me from crime.

CHORUS.

Father have mercy, Father have mercy, Father have mercy thro' Jesus christ our Lord.

Father have mercy &c.

2

Father in heaven, Oh! hear when we call,
Hear for Christ's sake who is Saviour of all,
Feeble and fainting we trust in thy might,
In doubting and darkness thy love be our light;
Let us sleep on Thy breast while the night taper burns,
And wake in thy arms when the morning returns.
Father have mercy &c, &c.

GENTLY, LORD, O GENTLY LEAD US.

— HYMN. —

Adapted to the Air of Absence, by T. Carr

Blake, Publisher Philada

Gent - ly, Lord, O gent - ly lead us, Thro' this lowly Vale of tears;

And, Oh Lord in mer - cy give us, Thy rich grace in all our fears:

Oh! re - fresh us, Oh! re - fresh us, Oh! re - fresh us with thy grace.

Interlude.

2
Though ten thousand ills beset us,
From without and from within;
Jesus says he'll ne'er forget us,
But will save from ev'ry sin.
|: Therefore praise him:|
Praise the great Redeemer's name.

3
Though distresses now attend thee,
And thou tread'st the thorny road,
His right hand shall still defend thee,
Soon he'll bring thee home to God.
|: Therefore praise him:|
Praise the great Redeemer's name.

SABBATH SCHOOL HYMN.

GIRLS.
BOYS.

Where do Children love to go, When the wint' - ry tempests blow,

Accomp.

What is it attracts them to? 'Tis the SABBATH SCHOOL.

Interlude.

2
When the Sabbath morning breaks,
Ev'ry eye from slumber wakes,
What so happy Children makes?
'Tis the SABBATH SCHOOL.

3
Where do pious Teachers stay,
From their peaceful homes away,
On the precious Sabbath day?
In the SABBATH SCHOOL.

4
Where are we so kindly taught,
God should rule in ev'ry thought,
What the blood of Christ has bought?
In the SABBATH SCHOOL.

5
May we ever love this day,
May we learn Salvation's way,
Love to read and sing and pray,
In the SABBATH SCHOOL.

HOME AGAIN

Words and Music by

MARSHALL S. PIKE ESQ.

SUNG WITH RAPTUROUS APPLAUSE BY THE

HARMONEONS

DEDICATED MOST AFFECTIONATELY TO

Lizzie C. Oakes

of Charlestown S.C.

ARRANGED FOR THE PIANO

— BY —

J. P. ORDWAY,

SONG 25 cts nett   QUARTETTE 25 cts nett

BOSTON *Published by* A & J. P. ORDWAY *339 Washington St.*
WATERS & BERRY *447 Broadway* NEW YORK

HOME AGAIN.

Words and music by M. S. Pike, Esq.   Arranged by J. P. ORDWAY.

Home a-gain, Home a-gain, from a foreign shore, And oh! it fills my soul with joy, To meet my friends once more; Here I drop'd the part-ing tear, To cross the ocean's foam, But now I'm once again with those, Who kind-ly greet me home!

Home a-gain, Home a-gain, from a foreign shore, And oh it fills my soul with joy, To

meet my friends once more,

Hap - py hearts, Hap - py hearts With mine have laugh'd in glee; But ah! the friends I lov'd in youth, Seem

hap - pier to me; And if my guide should be the fate Which bids me longer roam; But death a-lone can break the tie; That binds my heart to home, Home a-gain.

Home a-gain, from a foreign shore, And oh it fills my soul with joy; To

meet my friends once more.

3

Music sweet, Music soft,
  Lingers round the place;
And oh; I feel the childhood charm,
  That time cannot efface;
Then give me but my homestead roof,
  I ll ask no palace dome;
For I can live a happy life,
  With those I love at home.

THE WORDS COPIED FROM THE NEW YORK MIRROR, WRITTEN BY

GEORGE P. MORRIS,

BY WHOM THIS SONG IS RESPECTFULLY DEDICATED TO

BENJAMIN M. BROWN. ESQ.

THE MUSIC BY

Henry Russell.

New York. Published by FIRTH & HALL,. N. 1, Franklin Sq.

270

WOODMAN SPARE THAT TREE.

Pr: 50.

Words by George P. Morris, Esq.   Music by Henry Russell.

Wood....man spare that tree; Touch not a sin...gle

bough; In youth it shelterd me, And

I'll protect it now; 'Twas my fore fa...ther's

hand That placed it near his cot, There,

wood....man, let it stand, Thy axe shall harm it

give this foolish tree ___ but Let that old oak

not!

Stand

That old fami...liar tree, Whose glo...ry and re...

my heart strings round the cling... close at thy bark old

nown Are 'spread o'er land and sea, And

friend here...Shall the wild bird sing and

Con anima.

wouldst thou hack it down? Wood-man, for- bear thy

Still thy branches bend as thee the storm thills

stroke! Cut not its earth, bound ties; Oh!

base and wood man leave the Spot while

Woodman spare.   *s.*

spare that aged oak, Now tow...ering to the skies!

3

When but an idle boy
  I sought its grateful shade;
In all their gushing joy
  Here, too, my sisters played.
My mother kiss'd me here;
  My father press'd my hand —
Forgive this foolish tear,
  But let that old oak stand!

But let that old oak stand!

4

My heart-strings round thee cling,
  Close as thy bark, old friend!
Here shall the wild-bird sing,
  And still thy branches bend.
Old tree! the storm still brave!
  And, woodman, leave the spot;
While I've a hand to save,
  Thy axe shall harm it not.

Woodman spare. 4.

Come ye disconsolate

A SACRED SONG

(Arranged and Dedicated to)

Mr George Dutton

By

D. DUTTON.

Philad.ᵃ Publi-hed by G.E.Blake, 13 south Fifth street.

Come ye dis-consolate, where e'er ye languish,

Come at the mercy seat, fer-vent-ly kneel. Here bring your wounded hearts,

Here tell your an — guish, Earth hath no sor — row that Heav'n cannot heal.

Soprano 1. & 2.

Here bring your wounded hearts, here tell your an — guish, Earth hath no sorrow that Heav'n cannot heal.

Here bring your wounded hearts, here tell your an — guish, Earth hath no sorrow that Heav'n cannot heal.

2d STANZA.

Joy of the desolate, light of the straying,
Hope, when all others die, fadeless and pure,
Here speaks the Comforter, in mercy saying
"Earth hath no sorrow that Heav'n cannot cure."

ADDITIONAL HYMN.

Father of mercies, when the day is dawning   Yes, thou art near me sleeping or waking,
Then will I pay my vows to thee;   Still doth thy love unchang'd remain,
Like incense wafted on the breath of morning   Where'er I wander, thy ways forsaking,
My heart-felt praise to thee shall be.   O lead me gently back again.

(Come ye disconsolate)

Hark! the Vesper Hymn is stealing,

A Popular Russian Air, from

MOORE'S NATIONAL MELODIES,

Arranged by

Sir John Stevenson Mus: Doc:

Nº 15   Philadelphia Published by G.E. Blake.

In Moderate Time.

TREBLE.

First Verse ...... Hark! the ves_per hymn is stealing   O'er the wa_ters   soft and clear:

Second Verse ...... Now, like moonlight waves retreat_ing   To the shore, it   dies along;

TREBLE.

Near_er yet and near_er pealing, Now it bursts up_on the ear, Ju_bi_la_te

Now, like angry sur_ges meeting, Breaks the mingled tide of song.

COUNTER.

Ju _ bi _ _ _ _ la _ _ te   A _ _ men   A _ _ men,   Ju_bi_la_te

TENOR.

Ju _ _ bi _ _ _ _ la _ _ te   A _ _ men   A _ _ men,   Ju_bi_la_te

BASS.

Ju _ _ bi _ _ _ _ la _ _ te   A _ _ men   A _ _ men,   Ju_bi_la_te

PIANO FORTE.

Ju_bi_la_te Ju_bi_la_te A_men. * Farther now, now farther stealing, Soft it fades up_
Hush! again, like waves retreating To the shore it

Ju_bi_la_te Ju_bi_la_te A_men, Ju _ _ bi _ _ la _ _ te A _ men

Ju_bi_la_te Ju_bi_la_te A_men, Ju _ _ _ bi _ _ _ la _ _ _ te A _ men

Ju_bi_la_te Ju_bi_la_te A_men. Ju _ _ bi _ _ _ la _ _ te A _ _ men

on the ear. Farther now, now farther stealing, Soft it fades up on the ear.
dies a_long. Hush! again, like waves retreating To the shore, it dies a_long.

A _ _ men. Ju _ _ bi _ _ _ la _ _ te A _ _ _ men A _ _ men.

A _ _ men. Ju _ _ bi _ _ _ la _ _ te A _ _ _ men A _ _ men,

A _ _ men. Ju _ _ bi _ _ _ la _ _ te A _ _ _ men A _ men,

* This passage is added to the original Air by Sir John Stevenson.

From Greenland's Icy Mountains,

A MISSIONARY HYMN,

By the late **Bishop Heber** of Calcutta.

Composed & Dedicated to

Miss Mary M. Howard

of Savannah, Georgia

By

Lowell Mason.

Philad.ª Published by G. E. Blake, 13 South Fifth Street.

MODERATO.

From Greenland's i_cy mountains, From India's coral strand _ Where Afric's sunny fountains Roll down their golden sand: From many an ancient river—, From many a palmy plain—, They call us to de___liv__er Their land from error's chain.

2.

What tho' the spicy breezes, blow soft o'er Ceylon's isle,
Tho' ev'ry prospect pleases, and only man is vile;
In vain with lavish kindness, the gifts of God are thrown,
The heathen in his blindness bows down to wood and stone.

3.

Shall we, whose souls are lighted by wisdom from on high,
Shall we to men benighted the lamp of life deny?
Salvation! O Salvation! the joyful sound proclaim,
Till earth's remotest nation has learnt Messiah's name.

4.

Waft, waft, ye winds, his story, and you, ye waters, roll,
Till like a sea of glory, it spreads from pole to pole;
Till o'er our ransom'd nature, the lamb, for sinners slain,
Redeemer, King, Creator, in bliss returns to reign.

From Greenland's

I WOULD NOT LIVE ALWAY,

Composed and respectfully dedicated
to the
REV. FREDERICK T. GRAY,
BY
GEORGE KINGSLEY.

BOSTON
PARKER & DITSON

I WOULD NOT LIVE ALWAY,

Composed and Arranged for Four Voices

With an accompaniment for the

Piano Forte

And respectfully dedicated to the

REV. FREDERICK T. GRAY

By

GEO. KINGSLEY.

BOSTON: Published by C. BRADLEE Washington Street.

4

Tenor.

* I would not live alway, I   ask not to stay Where storm after storm rises dark o'er the way.

2d.Trebl:

I would not live alway, I   ask not to stay Where storm after storm rises dark o'er the way.

1st.Trebl:

I would not live alway, I   ask not to stay Where storm after storm rises dark o'er the way.

Bass .

PIANO FORTE.

Are enough for life's woes, full enough for its cheer.

The few lucid moments that dawn on us here, Are enough for life's woes, full enough for its cheer.

Are enough for life's woes, full enough for its cheer.

⊕ I would not live alway. I ask not to stay
Where storm after storm rises dark o'er the way.
I would not live alway, no, welcome the tomb,
Since Jesus hath lain there, I dread not its gloom.

* With Alterations.
⊕ Original.

Who, who would live alway a - way from his God, Away from yon heaven, that blissful abode!

Who, who would live alway a - way from his God, Away from yon heaven, that blissful abode!

Who, who would live alway a - way from his God, Away from yon heaven, that blissful abode!

And the noontide of glory eternally reigns

Where the rivers of pleasure flow o'er the bright plains And the noontide of glory eternally reigns

And the noontide of glory eternally reigns

Peds.

Where the saints of all ages in harmony meet,
Their Saviour and brethren transported to greet;
While the anthems of rapture unceasingly roll,
And the smile of the Lord is the life of the soul.

Watchman tell us of the Night

A Missionary or Christmas Hymn by
BOWRING

Sung at the Monthly Concert Park St. Church Boston

Music by
LOWELL MASON.

BOSTON: Published by C. BRADLEE   Washington Street.

Watchman! tell us of the night, What its signs of promise are; Trav'ller! o'er yon mountain's height, See that glo——ry beaming star! Watchman! does its beauteous ray Aught of hope or joy foretel? Trav'ller! yes; it brings the day, Promis'd day of Is—ra—el!

CHORUS.

1st Voice.

Watchman! yes, it brings the day,— Promis'd day of Is__ra__el!

2d Voice.

Trav'ller! yes, it brings the day,— Promis'd day of Is__ra__el!

Bass.

Trav'ller! yes, it brings the day,— Promis'd day of Is__ra__el!

Piano -
Forte.

8va.

Sym:

2.

Watchman! tell us of the night,
Higher yet that star ascends:
Trav'ller! blessedness and light
Peace and truth, its course portends,
Watchman! will its beams alone
Gild the spot that gave them birth?
Trav'ller! ages are its own,
See! it bursts o'er all the earth.

3.

Watchman! tell us of the night,
For the morning seems to dawn:
Trav'ller! darkness takes its flight,
Doubt and terror are withdrawn,
Watchman! let thy wand'rings cease;
Hie thee to thy quiet home:
Trav'ller! lo! the Prince of Peace,
Lo! the Son of God is come.

CHORUS to third Verse.

ff

Watchman! lo! the Prince of Peace, Lo! the Son of God is come! Lo! the Son of God is come!

ff

Trav'ller! lo! the Prince of Peace, Lo! the Son of God is come! Lo! the Son of God is come!

ff

Trav'ller! lo! the Prince of Peace, Lo! the Son of God is come! Lo! the Son of God is come!

f

ff

8va.

Sym: as above

www.ingramcontent.com/pod-product-compliance
Lightning Source LLC
Chambersburg PA
CBHW021533270326
41930CB00008B/1227